THE ULTIMATE PRAYER JOURNAL TO PREPARE FOR THE
INEVITABLE AND EXPLORE THE POSSIBLE

D0002115

Dig the Well Before You Get Thirsty

MATTHEW KELLY

BLUE SPARROW
North Palm Beach, Florida

Copyright © 2020
Kakadu, LLC
Published by Blue Sparrow

All rights reserved.
No part of this book may be used or reproduced in any
manner whatsoever without permission except in the case of
brief quotations in critical articles or reviews.

For more information, visit:
www.BlueSparrowBooks.org
www.MatthewKelly.com

ISBN: 978-1-63582-170-3 (softcover)

Designed by Ashley Wirfel

10   9   8   7   6   5   4   3   2   1

FIRST EDITION

Printed in the United States of America

Nothing will change your life so completely, absolutely, and forever like really learning how to pray.

From *I Heard God Laugh*

TABLE OF CONTENTS

INTRODUCTION

Are You Ready for a Life-Changing Experience?   4

PART **1**   *21 Questions that Will Change Your Life*   11

PART **2**   *What is God Saying To You Today?*   37

PART **3**   *A Journey Through I Heard God Laugh*   79

PART **4**   *The Discernment Process*   113

PART **5**   *Dreaming With God*   207

Are You Ready for a Life-Changing Experience?

Maybe you are, maybe you're not. Perhaps you think your life is just fine the way it is, or perhaps you are finally ready to face the dissatisfaction in your life. Wherever you are in your journey, I do believe that you are holding this journal in your hand at this moment for a reason. It's amazing how one choice can change the whole course of the rest of our lives. Choose to throw yourself into this experience, and I promise it will take you on an adventure that is, at this moment, a complete mystery to you.

CONNECTION WITH GOD

The book you are holding in your hands can change your life completely and forever. I am confident of that. Though it is less about the book and more about the inner work, this journal will lead you and will transform you and your life.

The goal is to rediscover—or perhaps discover for the very first time—your spiritual self, and to establish a vibrant connection with God.

Feelings aren't everything in the spiritual life, but they are also not nothing. Feeling connected with God is among the most profound experiences a human being can have. Many have experienced this, millions have not, and I believe it is largely because they have never been taught the things in this journal and its companion book and video series, *I Heard God Laugh*.

When we lose our connection with the Divine we go mad. When we lose our connection with God, we become alienated not only from God, we also become alienated from our very self.

Our common yearning is to explore and embrace the possibilities and potential that God has placed with us. Most people pass through life oblivious to the possibilities and disappointing their God-given potential, because they have not been taught how to do the inner work necessary to discover who they are, what they are here for, what matters most, and what matters least. Without a rich inner life, two essential practical functions become distorted: establishing priorities and making choices. With the wrong priorities, we inevitably make poor choices, and from there, life can easily become disappointing, boring, a drudgery, meaningless, depressing, and overwhelming.

And so, it becomes clear that connection with God and connection with our own self are essential to human flourishing. But they do not just happen. Connecting with God requires a proactive and consistent effort, and it requires sorting through our hearts, minds, and souls, to discern what truly is part of who we are and what baggage and burdens have been heaped upon us by others along the way.

Spring cleaning our hearts, minds, and souls is a process that takes time, needs to be revisited regularly, and is always worth it.

TWO QUESTIONS THAT WOKE ME UP

Some people come into our lives and remain, other people come into our lives for a wonderful season and then life draws them in a new direction, and still others, cross our path for just a moment.

A few years ago, I was asked two questions that stopped me in my tracks and really challenged me to reconsider the way I was living my life.

The first question was asked of me by a complete stranger. We met and chatted for less than five minutes, but as he turned to leave he asked me a rhetorical question: When was the last time you felt amazing?

I have not seen the man since. He crossed my path for just a moment, and in that moment he made a profound contribution to my journey simply by asking a question.

The second question was asked of me by a long-time friend. We were having one of our long chats, talking about the various things going on in our lives, and then our conversation wandered into a long pause. We both sat there in silence as we often do, reflecting on what we had been discussing, comfortable enough with each other for the quiet not to feel awkward. After about fifteen minutes, my friend looked up at me and asked: Do you feel like you are doing enough?

I don't think I have ever felt like I was doing enough. It isn't that I felt like I wasn't doing enough, but rather that I had never in more than 40 years of life on this earth paused to ask the question. At the same time, for my entire adult life, I had been constantly committed to doing more. In the days, weeks, months, and years that have followed I have spent a thousand hours pondering this single question. I have discussed it with friends and colleagues. I have gone deep within to explore the insecurity behind my ongoing compulsion to do more.

That question changed my life. It continues to change my life. It teaches me new things every time I sit with it. It teaches me about life, and it teaches me about myself. One of its latest lessons: It's possible to be doing too much and, at the same time, too little of the things that matter most.

Two questions. I could have waved them away like a fly at a barbeque on a hot summer's day. But by some grace they penetrated my resistance and my ego, and I was able to reflect on them.

I share them with you now because I want you to know that your life can be amazing, and that like most people, you are probably doing too much and at the same time neglecting some things that are critical if you are going to flourish.

What I know for sure, is that your life won't be amazing for any prolonged period of time without a disciplined daily routine of prayer and reflection. The other thing I know for sure, is that you won't be focused on doing enough of the things that matter most without a disciplined daily routine of prayer and reflection.

I know you are busy. We all are. But prayer allows us to trade in busy, anxious, overwhelmed, stressed, and worried in exchange for being fully engaged in the present moment. And that's a trade worth making.

Life is different with prayer, and a life with prayer is different.

Albert Einstein once remarked, "If I had an hour to solve a problem and my life depended on the solution, I would spend the first 55 minutes determining the proper question to ask. For once I know the proper question, I could solve the problem in less than five minutes."

The time it takes to get clarity about ourselves and our lives is invaluable. It is worth the time. It is worth making it a priority. Set aside some specific time for prayer and reflection each day, commit it to your schedule, and honor yourself and God by honoring that commitment. It will change your life, I can promise you that. I have experienced it myself and witnessed it in thousands of other people's lives.

THE PLACE TO START

A tree with deep roots can weather any storm. We all experience storms in our lives. It is not a question of whether or not we will experience another storm. That is not the question, but rather, when will the next storm be approaching? And when the storm arrives, it is too late
for a tree to sink roots. When the storm arrives, it either has the roots or it does not.

I have been battered around in the storms of life in both scenarios. For some of life's storms I was caught off guard and unprepared, and those storms damaged me significantly. But I have also encountered storms at times in my life when I was firmly committed to the daily routines of the spiritual life. These storms did nowhere near as much damage.

The storms you have experienced in life have passed. You can do nothing to prepare for them or to change them. You may be still picking up the wreckage that those storms unleashed in your life.

There will be more storms in your life. I don't know what and I don't know when, but they will come for they are part of every person's experience of life.

So begin to prepare today for the coming storms. Begin to develop deep roots by fostering a rich inner-life. Foster a rich inner-life by committing yourself to a daily routine of prayer and reflection.

I recommend three practices to ground your daily prayer and reflection:

1. **The Prayer Process**, which is explained in detail in *I Heard God Laugh* and the video series that accompanies this journal. It can also be found toward the end of this book.
2. **Daily Journaling**, which you will experience in a variety of ways through this journal.
3. **Spiritual Reading**, because books change our lives, because we become the books we read. Visit **MatthewKelly.com/reading** for a list of books that have fed my soul and changed my life.

Why does it matter? Why is it important for each of us to establish a daily routine of prayer and reflection?

When Jesus was on the cross, he cried out, "I thirst." In response to his desperate plea the soldiers gave him wine mixed with gall. This bitter combination would have only increased his dehydration and added to his misery.

I meet people every day who are crying out, "I thirst." And the world gives them wine mixed with gall, which only increases their dehydration and adds to their misery.

We are each thirsty in our own ways today. You know your thirst, and I know mine. Your thirst may be different next week, and it may be the same. But the reality is our souls are thirsty. And we cannot satisfy a spiritual thirst with a worldly potion.

Dig The Well Before You Get Thirsty. I chose this title because our spiritual thirst is real and isn't going away. Every day we are blessed to be on this earth, we will have a need to drink the living waters that God wants to freely give us. But we have to dig the well. How? By developing a daily practice of prayer and reflection. That's how we dig the well. That's how we gain access to the living water that Jesus spoke about.

Most people in our culture today are severely spiritually dehydrated. You may be in that place yourself. If you are, do not be discouraged, but don't be a victim either. Start digging your well today. Find a quiet place, sit with God, and pour your heart out to him. He will comfort you in your afflictions and afflict you in your comfort. He will encourage you and challenge you, but most of all, he will love you. And his love and acceptance will hydrate your soul like never before.

BE BOLD, BEGIN TODAY

There is boldness in resolve and boldness in action. Seize this moment to begin. Do not say, "I will start tomorrow." Begin today.

Will it be easy? No. It will be difficult. It may be the most difficult thing you have ever done. All the energy and enthusiasm you have for it some days will not be there on other days, and you will need to force yourself to take the time to connect with God. After years of being faithful every day to your daily routine, you may suddenly find yourself struggling. It is difficult in different ways for different people, but it is difficult for everyone. It's hard to get started, and it's hard to keep going. But it's worth it.

This is the main reason we don't pray, because it is difficult. The main reason we don't develop rich and vibrant inner lives is because it is difficult.

It's also the main reason people don't save money, the main reason people don't exercise regularly, the main reason people don't eat a balanced and healthy diet, and the main reason people don't do most of the things that would help them become a-better-version-of-themselves and live a richer, fuller life.

But life wasn't meant to be easy. This is one of the great fallacies in our minds that has us on an endless quest for comfort and ease. Our quest for ease and comfort is killing us, body and soul. Life is difficult. Anybody who tells you otherwise is not to be trusted.

Will establishing a daily habit of prayer and reflection be easy? Absolutely not. In fact, it might be the most difficult and satisfying, frustrating and exhilarating habit you every work to establish in your life. It is the most difficult thing I have ever done, and it remains difficult on many days.

But here's the thing. I am never sorry I did it. On days when I just don't feel like praying and I have to force myself to do it, when I am done, I am always glad I did.

So, begin today. Within these pages you will find five sections. Each section is designed to feed your heart, mind, and soul and build your connection with God like never before.

I encourage you to take 30 minutes each day to pray and reflect throughout this process. Using ten minutes of that time to practice The Prayer Process and the other twenty minutes to reflect and journal.

The five parts are each unique and designed to provide a variety of ways to reflect and journal with God. They can be experienced in whatever order you feel drawn to them.

I would like to suggest that you experience each of them more than once. For example, in part one as you consider the 21 questions, jot down your answers and date them. You may come back months or years from now and answer the same question in a different way. Comparing your answers at different times provides astounding insight into how God is working in us.

Watching God work in this way over time is one of the most illuminating and rewarding aspects of the spiritual life. Day-by-day, God points out the patterns in our lives—those that are life-giving and those that are soul-destroying.

Little by little, you will begin to live in your God-given strength. You will wake up one day and no longer feel tired, weak, and overwhelmed. You will have traded chaos for order, and confusion for clarity. You will feel free to say no, and thus, you will be free to say yes.

And on that day, you will decide, once and for all, never to live without prayer again. I will be praying with the Father, the Son, the Holy Spirit, and all God's angels and saints, that that day comes soon.

MATTHEW KELLY

" Wherever you are, whatever you're feeling, however life has surprised and disappointed you, I want to remind you of one thing: The best is yet to come!

Part One:

21 Questions that Will Change Your Life

THIS JOURNEY is about allowing God to teach us about ourselves. The word education comes from the Latin word *educare*, which means to draw out. So much of modern education is based on imposing knowledge upon us, stuffing us full of information. But the best teachers have always been focused on drawing something out of the student. The best teachers draw out the-best-version-of-ourselves. They make us more of who we truly are.

Since Socrates and Plato, the greatest teachers have not used a lecture method, but rather a method of questions and dialogue. Everything good and true and beautiful has its roots in God, and thus we discover, in many ways throughout our lives through people, experiences, and opportunities, God is laying questions before us. Always the right question at the right time, if we listen closely. At the same time there are many other people and voices in your life proposing different questions.

The questions we choose to focus on can make all the difference.

The questions we ponder determine the quality of our lives. Ponder trivial and shallow questions and your life is likely to become just that. Spend your days pondering questions that challenge you to explore yourself, others, the world, God, and spirituality in new and exciting ways, and you will live a life uncommon.

I have often said that if you tell me the books you are going to read over the next 12 months, I can probably tell you how your life will change in the next year. The reason is because we become the books we read.

Questions have a similarly powerful effect on the direction and trajectory of our lives. A person who spends the next year pondering, "Should I get divorced?" will have a radically different experience than the person who focuses on the question, "What can I do to renew and transform my marriage?"

The questions we ask of ourselves, of others, of life, and of God have a profound and mysterious impact on our lives.

We are impatient and like the gratification of quick answers, but they do not satisfy. The most important answers are those that we wrestle with. The reason is because we yearn for deeply personal answers to our deeply personal questions. You have to dig long and hard to find many of those answers, but they are worth the soul-work they require.

Be patient with your questions. Nobody has explained this more eloquently than Rainier Maria Rilke: "Be patient toward all that is unsolved in your heart and try to love the questions themselves, like locked rooms and like books that are now written in a very foreign tongue. Do not now seek the answers, which cannot be given you because you would not be able to live them. And the point is, to live everything. Live the questions now. Perhaps you will then gradually, without noticing it, live along some distant day into the answer."

I LAY BEFORE YOU HERE TWENTY-ONE QUESTIONS. Some will intrigue you more than others, but stretch your soul, and try to write down some answer for each question no matter how short. And date your answer. Then come back again, in weeks or months, and answer them again.

Don't be in a rush to answer the questions. Sit with them. Go deep into the questions. Answer them, and then answer them again. Date them. Come back to them. Add to them. When you add something, date the additions.

This is not because you will change your mind. The process is more profound than that. You will discover deeper parts of yourself. As you discover your deeper needs, talents, hopes, desires, and dreams, it is natural that your answers to many of life's most important questions will change.

The questions on these pages are simply designed to begin the process. They will fan the fire in your heart, and you will begin to recognize the questions being posed to you in the midst of your everyday activities.

Some questions are big picture, and some questions are nuts and bolts practical. Both are necessary. Some questions are beautiful, and some questions are ugly. If we are to thrive and grow, we need to face both with courage. But all in all, as we do this soul-work, our questions should become ever more beautiful.

EPHESIANS 3:20

Now to him who by the power at work within us is able to accomplish abundantly far more than all we can ask or imagine, to him be glory in the church and in Christ Jesus to all generations, forever and ever. Amen.

When was the last time you felt really amazing, and what would have to happen to get you back to that place?

Make a list of people you interact with frequently.
How is each helping you become the best version of yourself
(or not)...and vice-versa?

JEREMIAH
29:11

For surely I know the plans I have for you, says the Lord, plans for your welfare and not for harm, to give you a future with hope.

What are you dissatisfied with? If a friend described that situation to you and asked for advice, how would you advise him/her?

How much of each twenty-four-hour period do you spend in the past, present, and future?

Words spoken by the wise bring them favor, but the lips of fools consume them.

What needs to be on your NOT TO-DO list?

SONG OF SONGS
4:7

You are altogether beautiful, my love; there is no flaw in you.

What is something you have to do, because if you don't, your soul will start to die?

He answered, "You shall love the Lord your God with all your heart, and with all your soul, and with all your strength, and with all your mind; and your neighbor as yourself."

If money was no object what would your daily routine look like?

If you had the opportunity to share a message with millions of people, what would you say?

ISAIAH 40:31

Those who wait for the Lord shall renew their strength; they shall mount up with wings like eagles; they shall run and not be weary; they shall walk and not faint.

GALATIANS
2:20

Does the way you spend your time align with who and what you value most?

It is no longer I who live, but it is Christ who lives in me. And the life I now live in the flesh I live by faith in the Son of God, who loved me and gave himself for me.

Who inspires you—living or dead—and do you
spend enough time with those people?

LUKE
1:37

For nothing will be impossible with God.

JOHN
20:29

Jesus said to him, "Have you believed because you have seen me? Blessed are those who have not seen and yet have come to believe."

How do you want your life to be different one year from now?

What expectations have been placed on you by others that you need to release yourself from?

JOHN
6:44

No one can come to me unless drawn by the Father who sent me; and I will raise that person up on the last day.

If your body could talk to you, what do you think it would say?

JOHN
14:6

Jesus said to him, "I am the way, and the truth, and the life.
No one comes to the Father except through me."

Are your "shoulds" getting in the way of
your growth and happiness? If so, how?

ISAIAH
40:28

Have you not known? Have you not heard? The Lord is the everlasting God, the Creator of the ends of the earth. He does not faint or grow weary; his understanding is unsearchable.

JOHN
3:16

For God so loved the world that he gave his only Son, so that everyone who believes in him may not perish but may have eternal life.

If you had to choose between losing all your memories and never being able to make new ones, which would you choose?

In what ways does your lifestyle promote (or detract from) your physical, emotional, intellectual, and spiritual well-being?

JOHN
8:32

And you will know the truth, and the truth will make you free.

Cast your mind to ten or twenty years from now...
What's the one thing that if you didn't at least try to accomplish,
you would always regret?

What are you avoiding, and how is it hurting you?

JOHN
14:14

If in my name you ask me for anything, I will do it.

ISAIAH
43:2

When you pass through the waters I will be with you; and through the rivers, they shall not overwhelm you; when you walk through fire you shall not be burned, and the flame shall not consume you.

What is "on hold" in your life, and how would addressing it change your life?

If you knew you only had one year to live, what would you spend the next year doing?

ISAIAH
65:24

Before they call I will answer, while they are yet speaking I will hear.

ISAIAH
46:4

Even to your old age I am he, even when you turn gray I will carry you. I have made, and I will bear; I will carry and will save.

How do your best days begin, and what's keeping you from beginning each day in that way?

Part Two: What is God Saying to You Today?

THROUGHOUT THE BIBLE we read about God communicating with people. God speaks! But for some reason we forget this, think he won't speak to us, pretend we didn't hear him, and are afraid to really listen.

Learning to listen to God is one of the most exciting aspects of the spiritual life. Is it sometimes clear as day? Yes. Is it sometimes like deciphering code? Yes. Do we get it wrong sometimes? Yes. Is that part of the journey? Yes.

God is talking to us all the time, the question is: Are you listening?

Most people are not listening to God's voice in their lives. Why? They have never been taught how to listen to God's voice in their lives. This is one of the travesties and tragedies of life in the modern world, even for those who take their faith seriously.

God is talking to us all the time, but even when we do hear him, we immediately begin to doubt—was that God or just thoughts in my mind?—all the time forgetting that sometimes God will use the very thoughts in your mind to communicate with you.

We place so many limitations on God. Among the most significant are our attempts to narrow God's interest in us and restrict the ways he communicates with us. But God's interest in you knows no bounds, and the ways he communicates with us are unlimited.

God is not just interested in the spiritual aspect of your being. He is not just interested in the moral and ethical aspects of your life. He is interested in you as a whole person. He is not just interested in the parts of your life that directly involve religion and spirituality. He is interested in your whole life.

And God speaks to us in an infinite number of ways. He speaks to us through the circumstances of our lives; through the things that energize or drain our energy; through other people and in the Scriptures; through our habits and emotions; through the gentle voice within; through our gratitude and dissatisfaction; and through nature. God harnesses books, movies, music, and events in the world to speak to us.

That stirring you get in your soul when you sense that something is unjust, that's God talking to you. On those days when you feel a little off, God is saying something to you. When you fall asleep during your prayer time, God is saying something to you.

Learning to hear God's voice in the midst of our busy, noisy lives is a challenge. This is why we need to set aside time each day for prayer and reflection. This dedicated time allows us to develop a strong connection with God.

Think of this connection for a moment as a radio signal. Some radio signals are stronger than others. Our daily commitment to prayer makes our connection stronger with each passing day. The stronger this signal gets, the more easily it will be able to cut through the hustle and bustle of your busy life. This is important because we make many decisions during the day that we need God to weigh in on. The biggest decision we can ponder during our times of prayer and reflection, but the smaller decisions often need to be made quickly. Decide today to commit yourself to developing a strong connection with God. The more you do, the more you will recognize his presence and promptings throughout the day.

A weak radio signal can easily be interfered with by other radio signals. And there are so many radio stations in your life. Your friends each have a station, your parents have a station, your fears have a station, all the worlds experts have a station, the media has a station . . . and all these other stations can easily drown out your connection with God unless you develop a strong connection.

Learning to hear God's voice in your life throughout the day is like having the ultimate friend, coach, consultant, advisor, and teacher always at your side.

Most of the problems in our lives are born from valuing the wrong people's advice and opinions and ignoring the advice and opinions of the Creator of the Universe. Whose opinion is most influential in your life?

Place God's advice and opinions at the center of your life and amazing things will begin to happen. Clarity will emerge from the chaos of your life, you will finally, once-and-for-all feel like you are enough, and here's my favorite part . . . you will begin to recover the parts of you that you lost along the way. I know. It's a beautiful idea—and it is true!

Allow God to put you back together again.

IN THIS SECTION of the journal, you will make a forty-day journey. Each day a question will be posed to you. Nine questions in all. They will be repeated throughout the forty days. The repetition is designed to invite you deeper and deeper into the question each time. The repetition also helps to unearth patterns in our lives.

If something happens once, it's an event. If something keeps happening, it is a pattern.

Patterns tell us a lot about who we are and what we value. The easiest patterns to track in our lives are what we spend our money on and what we give our time to. We can learn an awful lot about ourselves just by exploring the patterns that surround our time and money. We can learn a lot about other people by observing their time and money patterns.

Patterns don't lie. We have healthy patterns and unhealthy patterns. Identifying them and talking with God about the impact they are having on our hearts, minds, bodies, and souls is essential to the journey. None of us can make progress without assessing and addressing our patterns.

So, when you happen upon the same question for the third or fourth time, resist the temptation to say, "I've done this already." Instead, go deeper into the question than ever before.

The last thing I will share with you as you embark on this journey is that nothing will weaken the signal and kill the connection like ignoring what you hear, and nothing will strengthen the signal and connection like living in God's guidance and direction. Each time God speaks to you, put what you hear into action. And each time you do, you will notice that his voice gets louder and clearer in your life. It may begin as a whisper, but the more you live what he says to you, the stronger his voice will become and the greater your joy.

What is God saying to you today...
through your current circumstances?

DAY

1

JEREMIAH
31:25

I will satisfy the weary, and all who are faint I will replenish.

JEREMIAH
33:3

Call to me and I will answer you, and will tell you great and
hidden things that you have not known.

What were you most energized about today . . .
and what is God saying to you through that?

What is God saying to you today...
through other people?

DAY

3

1 JOHN
4:7-8

Beloved, let us love one another, because love is from God; everyone who loves is born of God and knows God. Whoever does not love does not know God, for God is love.

Blessed are those who trust in the Lord, whose trust is the Lord.

What is God saying to you today . . .
about your habits?

What is God saying to you today through the emotions you are experiencing?

JEREMIAH
30:17

For I will restore health to you, and your wounds I will heal, says the Lord.

JEREMIAH
1:19

They will fight against you; but they shall not prevail against you, for I am with you, says the Lord, to deliver you.

What is God saying to you today . . .
through the gentle voice within you?

What are you grateful for today . . .
and what is God saying to you through that?

JEREMIAH
31:3

I have loved you with an everlasting love;
therefore I have continued my faithfulness to you.

The steadfast love of the Lord never ceases, his mercies never come to an end. They are new every morning; great is thy faithfulness.

What is God saying to you today . . .
about holding on and letting go?

What is God saying to you today . . .
through nature?

The Lord is good to those who wait for him, to the soul that seeks him.

What is God saying to you today . . .
through your current circumstances?

*What were you most energized about today . . .
and what is God saying to you through that?*

EZEKIEL
36:26

A new heart I will give you, and a new spirit I will put within you; and I will remove from your body the heart of stone and give you a heart of flesh.

I will send down the showers in their season; they shall be showers of blessing.

What is God saying to you today . . .
through other people?

What is God saying to you today . . .
about your habits?

DANIEL
11:32

The people who are loyal to their God shall stand firm and take action.

Do not fear, greatly beloved, you are safe. Be strong and courageous!

What is God saying to you today . . .
through the emotions you are experiencing?

What is God saying to you today . . .
Through the gentle voice within you?

HEBREWS 12:1

Therefore, since we are surrounded by so great a cloud of witnesses, let us also lay aside every weight and the sin that clings so closely, and let us run with perseverance the race that is set before us.

What are you grateful for today . . .
and what is God saying to you through that?

What is God saying to you today . . .
about holding on and letting go?

HOSEA
12:6

As for you, return to your God, hold fast to love and justice,
and wait continually for your God.

Return to the Lord, your God, for he is gracious and merciful, slow to anger, and abounding in steadfast love.

What is God saying to you today . . .
through nature?

What is God saying to you today . . . through your current circumstances?

1 TIMOTHY
6:12

Fight the good fight of the faith; take hold of the eternal life, to which you were called.

DAY
20

2 CHRONICLES
15:7

Take courage! Do not let your hands be weak, for your work shall be rewarded.

What were you most energized about today . . .
and what is God saying to you through that?

What is God saying to you today . . .
through other people?

PSALM
6:25

For God alone my soul waits in silence, for my hope is from him.
He alone is my rock and my salvation, my fortress; I shall not be shaken.

PSALM
86:5

For thou, O Lord, are good and forgiving, abounding in steadfast love to all who call on you.

What is God saying to you today . . .
about your habits?

What is God saying to you today . . .
Through the emotions you are experiencing?

DAY

23

PSALM
34:4-5

I sought the Lord, and he answered me, and delivered me from all my fears.
Look to him, and be radiant; so your faces shall never be ashamed.

But you, O Lord, are a shield around me, my glory, and the one who lifts up my head.

What is God saying to you today . . . through the gentle voice within you?

What are you grateful for today . . .
and what is God saying to you through that?

MATTHEW
11:29

Take my yoke upon you, and learn from me; for I am gentle and humble in heart, and you will find rest for your souls.

PSALM
94:18

When I thought, "My foot is slipping," your steadfast love, O Lord, held me up.

What is God saying to you today . . .
about holding on and letting go?

What is God saying to you today . . . through nature?

NEHEMIAH
8:10

For this day is holy to our Lord; and do not be grieved, for the joy of the Lord is your strength.

The Lord is my shepherd, I shall not want; he makes me lie down in green pastures. He leads me beside still waters; he restores my soul. He leads me in paths of righteousness for his name's sake.

What is God saying to you today . . .
through your current circumstances?

What were you most energized about today . . .
and what is God saying to you through that?

What is God saying to you today . . . through other people?

What is God saying to you today . . .
about your habits?

PSALM
37:5

Commit your way to the Lord; trust in him, and he will act.

What is God saying to you today . . .
through the emotions you are experiencing?

What is God saying to you today . . .
Through the gentle voice within you?

JOB
36:5

Surely, God is mighty, and does not despise any; he is mighty in strength of understanding.

The spirit of God has made me, and the breath of the Almighty gives me life.

*What are you grateful for today . . .
and what is God saying to you through that?*

What is God saying to you today . . .
about holding on and letting go?

I keep the Lord always before me; because he is at my right hand, I shall not be moved.

Take action, for it is your duty, and we are with you; be strong, and do it.

What is God saying to you today . . . through nature?

What is God saying to you today . . .
Through your current circumstances?

PSALMS
27:12

The LORD is my light and my salvation; whom shall I fear?
The LORD is the stronghold of my life; of whom shall I be afraid?

A cheerful heart is a good medicine, but a downcast spirit dries up the bones.

What were you most energized about today . . .
and what is God saying to you through that?

What is God saying to you today . . .
Through other people?

DAY

39

1 CHRONICLES
16:11

Seek the Lord and his strength, seek his presence continually!

O give thanks to the Lord, for he is good; for his steadfast love endures forever!

What is God saying to you today . . .
about your habits?

Part Three:

A Journey through

I Heard God Laugh

HOW DO YOUR BEST DAYS BEGIN?

My best days begin with prayer and reflection. It is such a simple discovery, but it took me many years to arrive at it. It is one of the absolute and undeniable truths of my life. And yet, there are still days when I rush headlong into my day without taking time to focus on what matters most.

I have tried a life grounded in prayer and reflection, and I have tried a life without prayer. I hope never to experience a life without prayer ever again. I simply do not know how people survive—never mind thrive—in this crazy, noisy, busy, distracting world, without some time each day in silence and solitude.

How do your best days begin? I have tried days with and without prayer, and the difference is epic. I encourage you to try both and observe the difference between a day that begins with prayer and reflection and one that doesn't.

Is it easy? Absolutely not. The daily habit of prayer requires, and is the result of, real spiritual work. It is incredibly difficult to establish a daily habit of prayer, and it is important that we are honest with ourselves and others about how difficult it is.

It is my own struggle that has taught me how very difficult it is to establish a daily habit of prayer, and how astoundingly difficult it is to access the discipline and wisdom to sustain that habit of prayer with unerring consistency.

When I wrote *I Heard God Laugh*, my only goal was to inspire you to develop or strengthen a daily habit of prayer. If I could give you any gift, I would give you this habit. Our lives change when our habits change. Nothing will change your life so completely and forever like really learning how to pray and establishing a daily habit of prayer in your life. It is life's quintessential habit. It is the quintessential life skill. But tragically, most of us pass through this world and never delve deeply into it.

No matter how old you are or how young you are, I encourage you to audit your spiritual life. Take an inventory of your character and virtue. Ask yourself if each day you are becoming more and more the person God created you to be. Wherever you are in the journey, I suspect such an assessment will inspire you to grow and change in new and wonderful ways. Prayer and reflection will allow God to bring those changes about in you.

The bottom line is this: Prayer makes me a better person. I am more generous, patient, compassionate, kind, thoughtful, and loving when my days are grounded in prayer from the start. Prayer makes me a better husband, father, brother, son, friend, colleague, leader, neighbor, citizen, and human being.

Prayer makes me better—and better, even just a tiny bit better, makes my soul dance for joy. And I want that for you. I have an agenda. It is this: that you discover the life-giving, soul-quenching, rejuvenating waters of prayer. I desire that deeply for you. It is a desire deeply rooted in love. Thomas Aquinas wrote, "Love is to will the good of the other," and nothing will awaken that goodness in you like daily prayer.

At this moment you are standing in the gap, between the past and the future, between the life that was and the life that still can be. No matter where you have been, no matter what you have done, place your friendship with God at the center of your life, and I can promise you that the best is yet to come. Give prayer priority in your life, and you will be amazed at just how delightful the rest of your life still can be.

🔍 *Today's Focus:*

When we reflect upon our lives, we usually discover that in some ways they are functioning well and in other ways they are dysfunctional.

📖 *Read:*

A Question to Begin from *I Heard God Laugh* beginning on page 3.

▶ *Watch:*

Video #1 at **IHeardGodLaugh.com**, and write down the one idea that resonates most with you.

_____

_____

_____

💡 *Reflect:*

"You can learn to live with your discontent, or you can accept it as an invitation." Is your life working? If your life isn't working, what are you willing to do about it?

_____

_____

_____

_____

_____

_____

_____

_____

_____

_____

🔍 Today's Focus:

There is no better time than right now to nurture your inner life, discover your spiritual needs, and feed your soul.

📖 Read:

The Missing Piece from *I Heard God Laugh* beginning on page 4.

▶ Watch:

Video #2 at **IHeardGodLaugh.com**, and write down the one idea that resonates most with you.

_____

_____

_____

💡 Reflect:

"The soul integrates and harmonizes every aspect of our humanity. It re-orients us toward what matters most." How well have you been taking care of your soul? Rate yourself between one and ten.

_____

_____

_____

_____

_____

_____

_____

_____

_____

🔍 *Today's Focus:*

Prayer helps us develop the awareness, virtue, and character that are essential when your life gets turned upside down.

📖 *Read:*

The Habit from *I Heard God Laugh* beginning on page 5.

▶ *Watch:*

Video #3 at **IHeardGodLaugh.com**, and write down the one idea that resonates most with you.

....

....

....

💡 *Reflect:*

"In prayer we learn how to love and be loved, because we discover that we have been loved, are loved, and will continually be loved by God." Has anyone ever taught you how to pray?

....

....

....

....

....

....

....

....

....

....

🔍 Today's Focus:

Prayer teaches us how to live and love.

📖 Read:

Finding Your Reason from *I Heard God Laugh* beginning on page 9.

▶ Watch:

Video #4 at **IHeardGodLaugh.com**, and write down the one idea that resonates most with you.

_____

_____

_____

💡 Reflect:

"Your questions are the gateway to the answers you seek. Treasure your questions." What attracts you to want to spend more time in prayer?

_____

_____

_____

_____

_____

_____

_____

_____

_____

_____

🔍 *Today's Focus:*

Habits unlock our potential, and no habit does this like daily prayer.

📖 *Read:*

Habit and Potential from *I Heard God Laugh* beginning on page 13.

▶️ *Watch:*

Video #5 at **IHeardGodLaugh.com**, and write down the one idea that resonates most with you.

....

....

....

💡 *Reflect:*

"God sees you and all your potential, and he aches to see you embrace your best, truest, highest self." In what ways have you yet to fully explore your potential?

....

....

....

....

....

....

....

....

....

....

....

Today's Focus:

It takes twenty-one days to establish a new habit in our lives, to sink its roots sufficiently so that the first strong breeze doesn't blow it away.

 ## Read:

The Challenge from *I Heard God Laugh* beginning on page 15.

Watch:

Video #6 at **IHeardGodLaugh.com**, and write down the one idea that resonates most with you.

Reflect:

"I invite you to reflect upon and take note of all the ways beginning your day with prayer has changed your life." How is your day different when you begin the day with prayer?

🔍 *Today's Focus:*

We often think of a conversion as a single decision or event, when the reality is that we are called to continuous conversion.

📖 *Read:*

The Invitation: Ten Minutes a Day from *I Heard God Laugh* beginning on page 20.

▶ *Watch:*

Video #7 at **IHeardGodLaugh.com**, and write down the one idea that resonates most with you.

....

....

....

💡 *Reflect:*

"Our lives seem to flood with grace at unexpected moments." What moments of transformation have you already experienced in your life?

....

....

....

....

....

....

....

....

....

....

....

🔍 Today's Focus:

There is one question that consistently leads to lasting happiness in this changing world: *God, what do you think I should do?*

📖 Read:

The First Surrender from *I Heard God Laugh* beginning on page 22.

▶ Watch:

Video #8 at **IHeardGodLaugh.com**, and write down the one idea that resonates most with you.

....

....

....

💡 Reflect:

"Peace comes from elevating the only opinion that truly matters: God's." When was the last time you invited God into a decision you were making?

....

....

....

....

....

....

....

....

....

....

....

Today's Focus:

The conversation with God about anything and everything that's happening in your life, about the things that are troubling you and the things that are bringing you joy, is at the heart of the spiritual life.

Read:

The Day My Life Changed Forever from *I Heard God Laugh* beginning on page 24.

Watch:

Video #9 at **IHeardGodLaugh.com**, and write down the one idea that resonates most with you.

....
....
....

Reflect:

"When God invites us to trust in him, he promises that everything will work out in the end, but he doesn't promise that everything will work out the way we want it to." How can you incorporate personal conversation with God into your life today?

....
....
....
....
....
....
....
....
....
....
....
....

🔍 Today's Focus:

"Teach us to pray" is the spoken and unspoken desire of every person, in every place and time. It reflects a desire for wisdom, which in turn reflects a desire to learn how to love and discover the best way to live.

📖 Read:

Teach Us to Pray from *I Heard God Laugh* beginning on page 35.

▶ Watch:

Video #10 at **IHeardGodLaugh.com**, and write down the one idea that resonates most with you.

_____

_____

_____

💡 Reflect:

"Birds were made to fly, fish were made to swim, and human beings were made to love God and each other." If God would grant you any one request, what would you ask him for?

_____

_____

_____

_____

_____

_____

_____

_____

_____

_____

🔍 *Today's Focus:*

The Prayer Process meets us where we are in the spiritual journey. Whether we have been praying every day for decades or just getting started, the Prayer Process meets us there and leads us gently, step-by-step, to become all God created us to be.

📖 *Read:*

Sharing the Joy from *I Heard God Laugh* beginning on page 37.

▶️ *Watch:*

Video #11 at **IHeardGodLaugh.com**, and write down the one idea that resonates most with you.

....

....

....

💡 *Reflect:*

"Never let what you can't do interfere with what you can do." How many minutes will you spend with the Prayer Process today?

....

....

....

....

....

....

....

....

....

....

....

🔍 Today's Focus:

The goal of the Prayer Process is to trigger a regular and meaningful conversation between you and God.

📖 Read:

The Prayer Process from *I Heard God Laugh* beginning on page 41.

▶ Watch:

Video #12 at **IHeardGodLaugh.com**, and write down the one idea that resonates most with you.

....

....

....

💡 Reflect:

"Prayer is about relationship, intimacy, and oneness with God. Conversation is at the heart of all dynamic relationships." What percentage of your daily activity are you conscious of? What percentage of your daily activity are you truly present to?

....

....

....

....

....

....

....

....

....

....

🔍 Today's Focus:

One of the great moments in the life of a Christian comes when we realize, once and for all, that a life with prayer is better than a life without prayer.

📖 Read:

Your Best Days from *I Heard God Laugh* beginning on page 45.

▶ Watch:

Video #13 at **IHeardGodLaugh.com**, and write down the one idea that resonates most with you.

....

....

....

💡 Reflect:

"Over time you will become more aware of how praying (or not praying) impacts you, your life, your relationships, your work, your health, your decisions, and every aspect of your day." How do your best days begin?

....

....

....

....

....

....

....

....

....

....

🔍 Today's Focus:

Success at almost anything rests upon this single principle: Do the basics, do them well, and do them every day, especially when you don't feel like doing them.

📖 Read:

The Basics from *I Heard God Laugh* beginning on page 48.

▶ Watch:

Video #14 at **IHeardGodLaugh.com**, and write down the one idea that resonates most with you.

_____

_____

_____

💡 Reflect:

"We allow ourselves to be seduced by the spectacular, but the basics are where you find the true and lasting treasure." In what areas of life are you seduced by the spectacular?

_____

_____

_____

_____

_____

_____

_____

_____

_____

_____

🔍 Today's Focus:

Through the daily habit of prayer and other spiritual practices, our image of God gradually becomes more aligned with the reality of who God is.

📖 Read:

What Is Your Image of God? from *I Heard God Laugh* beginning on page 51.

▶ Watch:

Video #15 at **IHeardGodLaugh.com**, and write down the one idea that resonates most with you.

_____

_____

_____

_____

💡 Reflect:

"Through a daily habit of prayer, we are seeking to experience the loving God who is love." What are three attributes that most help you connect with God?

_____

_____

_____

_____

_____

_____

_____

_____

_____

_____

_____

_____

Today's Focus:

Finding the name that best helps you to connect with God and enter into conversation with him is essential to establishing a vibrant life of prayer.

Read:

There Is Power in a Name from *I Heard God Laugh* beginning on page 56.

Watch:

Video #16 at **IHeardGodLaugh.com**, and write down the one idea that resonates most with you.

_____

_____

_____

Reflect:

"Our relationship with God should be by its very nature dynamic: positive, full of life and energy, changing and growing, a force that stimulates change and progress." What name best helps you enter into conversation with God?

_____

_____

_____

_____

_____

_____

_____

_____

_____

_____

🔍 Today's Focus:

Let your habit of daily prayer be the beginning of many powerful new routines in your life, so you may flourish like never before.

📖 Read:

Begin Today from *I Heard God Laugh* beginning on page 60.

▶ Watch:

Video #17 at **IHeardGodLaugh.com**, and write down the one idea that resonates most with you.

_____

_____

_____

💡 Reflect:

"God is constantly inviting us to grow, to develop, to change, to love more deeply, and to become the whole person he created us to be. This requires daily conversion of the heart." Have you begun a habit of daily prayer yet? If not, what are you waiting for?

_____

_____

_____

_____

_____

_____

_____

_____

_____

_____

🔍 Today's Focus:

Prayer helps us make the journey from the head to the heart, and it is prayer that allows us to balance the heart and mind so that we can live in wisdom.

📖 Read:

The Longest Journey and *Six Seismic Shifts* from *I Heard God Laugh* beginning on page 66.

▶ Watch:

Video #18 at **IHeardGodLaugh.com**, and write down the one idea that resonates most with you.

....

....

....

💡 Reflect:

"The significant moments on the pilgrimage of our lives usually present us with a choice that needs to be made." Are you living your life from your mind? Or are you living your life from your heart?

....

....

....

....

....

....

....

....

....

🔍 Today's Focus:

This first shift requires us to make the journey from the head to the heart, to turn from a thinking type of prayer to a relational style of prayer.

📖 Read:

The First Shift: Begin the Conversation from *I Heard God Laugh* beginning on page 68.

▶ Watch:

Video #19 at **IHeardGodLaugh.com**, and write down the one idea that resonates most with you.

....

....

....

💡 Reflect:

"Once the conversation has begun, it can lead anywhere. Most important, it will lead to the places it needs to lead to." What will you converse with God about today?

....

....

....

....

....

....

....

....

....

....

....

....

🔍 Today's Focus:

When we start asking God for advice, direction, inspiration, and guidance, this is a significant moment.

📖 Read:

The Second Shift: Ask God What He Wants from *I Heard God Laugh* beginning on page 69.

▶ Watch:

Video #20 at **IHeardGodLaugh.com**, and write down the one idea that resonates most with you.

....

....

....

💡 Reflect:

"This curiosity about God and his dreams for us and the world can be incredibly invigorating. It transforms the way we see ourselves, other people, creation, society, and indeed God." In what area of your life do you need to ask for God's advice, direction, or inspiration?

....

....

....

....

....

....

....

....

....

....

🔍 Today's Focus:

Giving yourself to prayer means showing up and letting God do what he wants to do with you during that time of prayer.

📖 Read:

The Third Shift: Give Yourself to Prayer from *I Heard God Laugh* beginning on page 71.

▶ Watch:

Video #21 at **IHeardGodLaugh.com**, and write down the one idea that resonates most with you.

_____

_____

_____

💡 Reflect:

"This shift requires us to surrender ourselves to the experience and to believe that God is working in us even when it feels like we are not accomplishing anything." Looking back on your life so far, in what ways and at what times are you able to recognize that God was at work in your life?

_____

_____

_____

_____

_____

_____

_____

_____

_____

_____

_____

🔍 Today's Focus:

Every honest human activity can be transformed into prayer.

📖 Read:

The Fourth Shift: Transform Everything into Prayer from *I Heard God Laugh* beginning on page 73.

▶ Watch:

Video #22 at **IHeardGodLaugh.com**, and write down the one idea that resonates most with you.

_____

_____

_____

💡 Reflect:

"Every moment is a precious gift, and the present moment is where God resides." Which of your daily activities will you ask God to help transform into prayer today?

_____

_____

_____

_____

_____

_____

_____

_____

🔍 Today's Focus:

Whatever space you make available to God, he will fill with unimaginably good things.

📖 Read:

The Fifth Shift: Make Yourself Available from *I Heard God Laugh* beginning on page 77.

▶ Watch:

Video #23 at **IHeardGodLaugh.com**, and write down the one idea that resonates most with you.

....

....

....

💡 Reflect:

"The joy we experience is proportional to how available we make ourselves to God." How available are you to God at this time in your life?

....

....

....

....

....

....

....

....

....

....

....

....

🔍 Today's Focus:

The sixth seismic shift occurs when showing up for our daily prayer is no longer a daily decision. It is a commitment, a decision that no matter what I am going to show up and be with God for that time each day.

📖 Read:

The Sixth Shift: Just Keep Showing Up! from *I Heard God Laugh* beginning on page 83.

▶ Watch:

Video #24 at **IHeardGodLaugh.com**, and write down the one idea that resonates most with you.

....

....

....

💡 Reflect:

"The only failure in prayer is to stop praying." How will you place the daily habit of prayer at the center of your life?

....

....

....

....

....

....

....

....

....

🔍 Today's Focus:

God does all the heavy lifting in the spiritual life. These are things that God does in us. All he asks us to do is open ourselves to him and cooperate.

📖 Read:

Six Life-Changing Awakenings from *I Heard God Laugh* beginning on page 83.

▶ Watch:

Video #25 at **IHeardGodLaugh.com**, and write down the one idea that resonates most with you.

....

....

....

💡 Reflect:

"Your journey will be as unique and different as a sunset." Who are the people in your life who help you remember what matters most?

....

....

....

....

....

....

....

....

....

....

....

Q Today's Focus:

God is the genius who is alive and well in laughter. Laughter is medicine for the mind, body, and soul. Its benefits are endless.

📖 Read:

Does God Have a Sense of Humor? from *I Heard God Laugh* beginning on page 89.

▶ Watch:

Video #26 at **IHeardGodLaugh.com**, and write down the one idea that resonates most with you.

....

....

....

💡 Reflect:

"Just as humor is essential to the human experience, it is also essential to our spiritual experience." Do you believe that God has a sense of humor?

....

....

....

....

....

....

....

....

....

....

....

....

🔍 Today's Focus:

The more we get to know God, the more we desire to know him.

📖 Read:

I Heard God Laugh from *I Heard God Laugh* beginning on page 93.

▶ Watch:

Video #27 at **IHeardGodLaugh.com**, and write down the one idea that resonates most with you.

....

....

....

💡 Reflect:

"Be still and quiet for long enough and God will reveal himself to you in ways you never dreamed." In what ways has God been preparing you for this season of your life and all that it involves?

....

....

....

....

....

....

....

....

....

....

....

Today's Focus:

The spiritual life is a constant invitation to go beyond the shallow and superficial offerings of this world and seek out the deep places.

Read:

The Deep Waters from *I Heard God Laugh* beginning on page 97.

Watch:

Video #28 at **IHeardGodLaugh.com**, and write down the one idea that resonates most with you.

....

....

....

Reflect:

"What we think about, reflect upon, and contemplate, has an enormous impact on the events of our lives and the state of our souls." How is God inviting you to go deeper in your spiritual life?

....

....

....

....

....

....

....

....

....

....

🔍 **Today's Focus:**

God delights in one thing above all else, and his delight teaches us some very powerful lessons. The delight of God is to be with his sons and daughters.

📖 **Read:**

The Delight of God from I Heard God Laugh beginning on page 100.

▶ **Watch:**

Video #29 at **IHeardGodLaugh.com**, and write down the one idea that resonates most with you.

....

....

....

💡 **Reflect:**

"When we invite God into our lives he dances for joy." Are you willing to let God take your prayer life to the next level? What makes you hesitant or resistant?

....

....

....

....

....

....

....

....

....

....

🔍 Today's Focus:

Prayer helps us to discern our true priorities and align our daily schedule with our discerned priorities.

📖 Read:

Busy Is Not Your Friend from *I Heard God Laugh* beginning on page 104.

▶ Watch:

Video #30 at **IHeardGodLaugh.com**, and write down the one idea that resonates most with you.

....

....

....

💡 Reflect:

"To live deeply and deliberately with focused intention, we need to assess the content of our lives." Is your life working?

....

....

....

....

....

....

....

....

....

....

Part Four:
The Discernment
Process

MOMENTS OF DECISION

Life is choices. We make hundreds of choices each day. Some big, some small. Some seem small at the time, but later, turn out to be life-changing.

God told Solomon he would give him anything. Solomon asked for wisdom. Why? So that he could make wise choices and decisions.

The one thing I have become convinced of over the years is that God wants to teach and train us to become phenomenal decision makers. Isn't that the dream of every parent—that their child makes good decisions?

Sooner or later, we all arrive at moments of decision that we know are important. What we do in those moments matters. And yet, when those moments arrive, most people feel unprepared. I don't know about you, but nobody ever taught me how to make great decisions. Sure, lots of people gave good and wise advice, but when the big moments arrived, I felt like I was clumsily juggling all these individual pieces of advice. I needed some system or process to pull them all together.

It was only when I began to explore the saints and mystics, that I discovered that there was an art to discernment and that it was an essential life-skill.

There are many reasons to begin digging the well today (or keep digging the well). The first is simply that you are going to get thirsty. It's inevitable. It's not something that might happen, it is something that is definitely going to happen. And preparing for the inevitable is just good old-fashioned common sense.

The other thing that is inevitable is that you are going to have decisions to make. Some of them big and important and life-changing. A deep spiritual well will almost certainly help you to make healthy, God-centered choices.

The deeper you dig your well with the daily habit of prayer and reflection, the easier it will be for you to tune into God during the moments in your life when you need to make decisions.

When moments of decision emerge, it's critical to remember that God wants to communicate with you. God communicates directly with each and every human heart. So, no matter how much you are yearning for God to speak to you, just know that he desires to speak with you more. No matter how far away God may seem at times, just know that he is closer than you think and yearns to be closer than ever.

How does God communicate with us? Through our dreams, sleeping and waking. Through our feelings, thoughts, desires, talents, and opportunities. Through the Scriptures and the life of the Church. Through other people and in the quiet of our hearts.

Most of what God is trying to communicate to us we miss. Why? Because we are tuned in to other messages and messengers. Learning to listen to the voice of God in our lives is one of the most ordinary and extraordinary aspects of the spiritual life. Ordinary because in any great relationship communication is one of the basics. Extraordinary because communicating with God is amazing.

Once we realize that we can communicate with God and that he desires to communicate with us, most people have questions. We may bring many questions and lay them before God, but discernment is ultimately about one question: What does God want us to do?

The two main reasons most people don't discover the will of God for their lives are (1) because they are not willing to follow and (2) because nobody ever taught them how to listen to his voice in their lives.

At the heart of discernment is a willingness to follow God. How often do children walk ahead of their parents, even though they have no idea where they are going? We do the same thing with God. He wants to take us on an amazing adventure and lead us to experience wonderful people, places, and things . . . but we are constantly getting distracted and wandering off.

Are you ready to follow God's lead? I hope so. I mean, let's face it, in the grand-scheme of things (and there is a grand-scheme), could there be anything more tragic than not discovering what God wants you to do with the rest of your life?

Moments of decision are inevitable. Life is full of opportunities, and therefore, full of choices to be made. No matter how young you are or how old you are, there is no better time than right now to learn to listen to God's voice in your life . . . or to tune back in.

Learning to follow God's lead is the project of our lives.

HOW TO USE THESE DISCERNMENT PAGES

Discerning the bigger questions in our lives usually requires time. For this section of this prayer journal, I suggest you take forty-days to discern a question. You may not have a big question to discern at this time of your life, and if that is the case, I suggest you wait for such a question to come along and use these pages and this process at that time.

The first rule of discernment is that you are always discerning between two good things, options or opportunities. Choosing between good and evil does not require discernment. It requires character.

In the pages that follow, you will find the outline of a forty-day discernment process. As you work your way through these pages there are going to be moments of great enthusiasm and moments of discouragement. There will be moments of clarity and moments of confusion. It's important that you remember that this inner struggle is natural and normal.

Ignatius of Loyola described two very specific states that our souls experience in our efforts to walk with God and discover his will for our lives. The first he called *Consolation*. When we experience consolation: we feel fully alive; we feel more connected to others; and, we feel that every part of our being is in harmony with God. The second is called *Desolation*. When we experience desolation: we feel restless, anxious, heavy, and discouraged; we experience doubts and temptations; we are easily distracted by the things of this world; and God can seem far away or even non-existent.

During times of consolation it is important to immerse yourself in the experience; realize that it is a gift you did nothing to cause; and be aware that it will not last for the rest of your life. During times of desolation it is important to be aware that it will not last indefinitely; focus on the basics of your spiritual life; keep showing up for your spiritual practices even when they feel like a waste of time; and trust that you are growing even though it seems impossible to believe at the time.

As you work your way through the forty-day process you will likely experience degrees of consolation and desolation. Remember that God can, and does, use both to communicate with us.

Before you set out on this journey, it is essential that you formulate the question that you are going to discern. The word "formulate" might seem out of place when talking about loving God and listening to his voice in your life. It isn't. It is absolutely critical that you formulate the question before setting out on this process of discernment. The reason is that, unless you do, you will likely change the question many times during the forty-days.

The question itself is of great importance. Spend some time thinking about it, praying about, and jotting down different versions if you need to.

Once you have established the question, write it down on the page provided. From that point on you will do the same exercises every day.

1. **Revisit the question each day before you begin journaling**. The heart and the mind have a tendency to change the question, and even a small shift can make a huge difference. Lay the same question before God each day, and spend some time in silence just sitting with God and your question.

2. **Begin with a Prayer of Gratitude**. Bring to mind the times in your past when you have felt that God was guiding or directing you, or times in your life that you realize looking back that God was watching out for you. Thank God for his love and direction.

3. **Gut Check**. What are you leaning toward today? If your question is a yes or no question, you can simply write yes or no. If your question is more involved, use as few words as possible to describe what you are leaning toward today in relation to the question you are discerning.

4. **Consolation and Desolation**. Does your soul feel light or heavy today?

5. **Feelings**. What is your dominant emotion today? Optimistic, pessimistic, enthusiastic, discouraged, happy, sad, angry, etc. Don't judge your feelings. We don't manufacture our feelings, they surprise us. Let them surprise you, and write them down.

6. **Heart**. What is your heart telling you to do? The heart often does not disclose its reasons. That's okay.

7. **Mind**. What is your mind telling you to do? The mind has reasons. What reasons do you believe are behind what your mind is telling you? Your reasons might be different every day. That's okay. Just write them down. The reasons may seem crazy to you. That's okay. Still write them down.

8. **Direction**. Where are you running? Do you feel like you are running toward something or away from something? Do you feel like you are running toward the-best-version-of-yourself or away from it? Again, your answer may change from day to day. That's okay. Keep writing it down.

9. **Motive**. Motives are a powerful force in our lives. What motive is driving you today? Just write it down. We always have more than one motive, but try to focus in on your dominant motive today. Whatever it is, write it down. Don't judge it, just write it down. The good, the bad, and the ugly. Write it down. Nobody has pure motives. Explore your motives for wanting to take that path. I say motives—plural —because we never have pure or singular motives. So, try to explore different motives on different days. Our hearts are complicated and often conflicted. It is not uncommon to have six or seven motives for wanting to do something. A young woman who chooses to become a doctor may have all of these motives: she is genuinely interested in medicine; she has a strong altruistic sense and wants to help others; she wants to have a successful career; she wants to make a good income; and, she wants to love and serve God by loving and serving others. All these motives can co-exist in one heart at the same time. None of these motives are bad. There are of course unhealthy motives and it is important to identify those also. For example, if the woman's dominant motive for wanting to become a doctor was to please her mother or father, this would be unhealthy and important to explore. It is when we don't acknowledge them that they grow dark and develop power over us.

10. **Anything else**. Write down any other thoughts or feelings that you have today about the question you are discerning.

Throughout this process you are encouraged to make written notes for two very specific reasons. First, the written notes make it much harder for us to confuse or deceive ourselves (or for any other person or spirit at work in our lives to confuse or deceive us). Second, the written notes make it easier to see the patterns as they emerge.

Patterns also play a crucial role in the discernment process. If at the end of forty-days, you felt called to act in one way thirty-seven out of the forty days, that is an important pattern. If you were evenly divided, feeling one way twenty days and the other way the other twenty days, you might not be ready to make the decision.

Learning to listen to the voice of God in our lives requires commitment and patience. Learning to discern his will for our lives requires an openness to grace. It helps to remember that we already know God's will in general, even if his specific will in a situation may be baffling us at the present moment.

In what ways do we already know the will of God? God desires good over evil, virtue over vice, and he wants you to become the-best-version-of-yourself, not a second-rate version. So, while we may be confused about what God wants us to do in a particular situation, it is important not to generalize this confusion and start to believe that we don't know his will at all. Because doing his will in the broadest definition is what usually leads us to clarity about his will in specific circumstances.

In the *Book of Micah*, we find another beautiful description of God's will: "He has told you, o people, what is good. And what does the Lord require of you: that you live justly, love tenderly, and walk humbly with your God" (Micah 6:8).

Learning to follow God's lead is the project of our lives. First and foremost, it requires the mindset of a humble follower. Pray that he gives you the grace, courage, and wisdom to follow and follow close to him. The other path is filled with pain and misery.

"

We have so many questions, and all too often we turn to the people around us as we look for answers, instead of turning to the one who has all the answers to all the questions. Your questions are the gateway to the answers you seek. Treasure your questions. Honor them enough to seek answers, and not just any answers. My sense is that you are not looking for generalized answers quoted to you from a book. You yearn for deeply personal answers to your deeply personal questions. The world cannot give you these. The people in your life cannot answer these questions for you, even those who know you and love you most. If you truly want to seek and find these answers, this is work for the soul. These are matters that are between you and God.

It takes courage to place our questions before God in prayer. It takes patience to wait for the answers, which are sometimes given to us in prayer and sometimes delivered through other people and the experience of daily life. It takes wisdom to live the answers we discover. I pray you are blessed with an abundance of courage, patience, and wisdom for the journey we are embarking upon.

From *I Heard God Laugh*

The Question

What question are you discerning
over the next forty days?

Trust in the Lord with all your heart, and do not rely on your own insight. In all your ways acknowledge him, and he will make straight your paths.

— Day One —

1. Revisit the Question.

2. Begin with a Prayer of Gratitude.

for the times God has guided you in the past.

3. Gut Check.

What are you leaning towards today?   **YES** ☐   **NO** ☐

4. Are you experiencing Consolation or Desolation Today?

Does your soul feel   **LIGHT**   *or*   **HEAVY**   today?

☐ **CONSOLATION**

☐ **DESOLATION**

5. Feelings.

What is your dominant emotion today?

6. Heart.

What is your heart telling you to do?

7. Mind.

What is your mind telling you to do?

8. Direction.

Do you feel like you are running toward something or away from something?

9. Motive.

What motive is driving you today?

10. Write down any other thoughts or feelings that you have today about the question you are discerning.

— Day Two —

1. Revisit the Question.

2. Begin with a Prayer of Gratitude.

for the times God has guided you in the past.

3. Gut Check.

What are you leaning towards today?   YES ☐   NO ☐

4. Are you experiencing Consolation or Desolation Today?

Does your soul feel   **LIGHT**   *or*   **HEAVY**   today?

☐ **CONSOLATION**

☐ **DESOLATION**

5. Feelings.

What is your dominant emotion today?

6. Heart.

What is your heart telling you to do?

JONAH 2:2

I called to the Lord out of my distress, and he answered me.

7. Mind.

What is your mind telling you to do?

_____

_____

_____

_____

8. Direction.

Do you feel like you are running toward something or away from something?

_____

_____

_____

_____

9. Motive.

What motive is driving you today?

_____

_____

_____

_____

10. Write down any other thoughts or feelings that you have today about the question you are discerning.

_____

_____

_____

_____

1 TIMOTHY
6:11

But as for you... pursue righteousness, godliness, faith, love, endurance, gentleness.

— Day Three —

1. Revisit the Question.

2. Begin with a Prayer of Gratitude.

for the times God has guided you in the past.

3. Gut Check.

What are you leaning towards today?   YES ☐   NO ☐

4. Are you experiencing Consolation or Desolation Today?

Does your soul feel   **LIGHT**   *or*   **HEAVY**   today?

☐ **CONSOLATION**

☐ **DESOLATION**

5. Feelings.

What is your dominant emotion today?

6. Heart.

What is your heart telling you to do?

7. Mind.

What is your mind telling you to do?

8. Direction.

Do you feel like you are running toward something or away from something?

9. Motive.

What motive is driving you today?

10. Write down any other thoughts or feelings that you have today about the question you are discerning.

1 TIMOTHY 4:12

Don't let anyone think less of you because you are young. Be an example to all believers in what you say, in the way you live, in your love, your faith, and your purity.

1 KINGS 2:3

Keep the charge of the Lord your God, walking in his ways and keeping his statutes, his commandments... that you may prosper in all that you do and wherever you turn.

1. *Revisit the Question.*

2. *Begin with a Prayer of Gratitude.*

for the times God has guided you in the past.

3. *Gut Check.*

What are you leaning towards today?   **YES** ☐   **NO** ☐

4. *Are you experiencing Consolation or Desolation Today?*

Does your soul feel   **LIGHT**   *or*   **HEAVY**   today?

☐ **CONSOLATION**

☐ **DESOLATION**

5. *Feelings.*

What is your dominant emotion today?

6. *Heart.*

What is your heart telling you to do?

7. Mind.

What is your mind telling you to do?

8. Direction.

Do you feel like you are running toward something or away from something?

9. Motive.

What motive is driving you today?

10. Write down any other thoughts or feelings that you have today about the question you are discerning.

2 KINGS
20:5

I have heard your prayer, I have seen your tears; indeed, I will heal you.

2 THESSALONIANS
3:3

But the Lord is faithful; he will strengthen you and guard you from evil.

— Day Five —

1. Revisit the Question.

2. Begin with a Prayer of Gratitude.

for the times God has guided you in the past.

3. Gut Check.

What are you leaning towards today?   YES ☐   NO ☐

4. Are you experiencing Consolation or Desolation Today?

Does your soul feel   **LIGHT**   *or*   **HEAVY**   today?

☐ **CONSOLATION**

☐ **DESOLATION**

5. Feelings.

What is your dominant emotion today?

6. Heart.

What is your heart telling you to do?

7. Mind.

What is your mind telling you to do?

8. Direction.

Do you feel like you are running toward something or away from something?

9. Motive.

What motive is driving you today?

10. Write down any other thoughts or feelings that you have today about the question you are discerning.

2 THESSALONIANS 3:16

Now may the Lord of peace himself give you peace at all times in all ways. The Lord be with you all.

2 THESSALONIANS
3:5

May the Lord direct your hearts to the love of God and to the steadfastness of Christ.

— Day Six —

1. Revisit the Question.

2. Begin with a Prayer of Gratitude.

for the times God has guided you in the past.

3. Gut Check.

What are you leaning towards today?   YES ☐   NO ☐

4. Are you experiencing Consolation or Desolation Today?

Does your soul feel   **LIGHT**   *or*   **HEAVY**   today?

☐ **CONSOLATION**

☐ **DESOLATION**

5. Feelings.

What is your dominant emotion today?

6. Heart.

What is your heart telling you to do?

7. Mind.

What is your mind telling you to do?

8. Direction.

Do you feel like you are running toward something or away from something?

9. Motive.

What motive is driving you today?

10. Write down any other thoughts or feelings that you have today about the question you are discerning.

AMOS
5:4

For thus says the Lord to the house of Israel: Seek me and live.

MICAH
7:7

But as for me, I will look to the Lord, I will wait for the God of my salvation; my God will hear me.

— Day Seven —

1. Revisit the Question.

2. Begin with a Prayer of Gratitude.

for the times God has guided you in the past.

3. Gut Check.

What are you leaning towards today?　　　YES ☐　　　NO ☐

4. Are you experiencing Consolation or Desolation Today?

Does your soul feel **LIGHT** *or* **HEAVY** today?

☐ **CONSOLATION**

☐ **DESOLATION**

5. Feelings.

What is your dominant emotion today?

6. Heart.

What is your heart telling you to do?

7. Mind.

What is your mind telling you to do?

8. Direction.

Do you feel like you are running toward something or away from something?

9. Motive.

What motive is driving you today?

10. Write down any other thoughts or feelings that you have today about the question you are discerning.

MICAH
6:8

He has told you, O mortal, what is good; and what does the Lord require of you but to do justice, and to love kindness, and to walk humbly with your God?

— Day Eight —

1. Revisit the Question.

2. Begin with a Prayer of Gratitude.

for the times God has guided you in the past.

3. Gut Check.

What are you leaning towards today?　　　YES ☐　　　　NO ☐

4. Are you experiencing Consolation or Desolation Today?

Does your soul feel　**LIGHT**　*or*　**HEAVY**　today?

☐ **CONSOLATION**

☐ **DESOLATION**

5. Feelings.

What is your dominant emotion today?

6. Heart.

What is your heart telling you to do?

7 Mind.

What is your mind telling you to do?

8. Direction.

Do you feel like you are running toward something or away from something?

9. Motive.

What motive is driving you today?

10. Write down any other thoughts or feelings that you have today about the question you are discerning.

EXODUS 23:25

You shall worship the Lord your God, and I will bless your bread and your water; and I will take sickness away from among you.

— Day Nine —

EXODUS 20:12

Honor your father and your mother, so that your days may be long in the land which the Lord your God is giving you.

1. Revisit the Question.

2. Begin with a Prayer of Gratitude.

for the times God has guided you in the past.

3. Gut Check.

What are you leaning towards today?   YES ☐   NO ☐

4. Are you experiencing Consolation or Desolation Today?

Does your soul feel   **LIGHT**   *or*   **HEAVY**   today?

☐ **CONSOLATION**

☐ **DESOLATION**

5. Feelings.

What is your dominant emotion today?

6. Heart.

What is your heart telling you to do?

7. Mind.

What is your mind telling you to do?

8. Direction.

Do you feel like you are running toward something or away from something?

9. Motive.

What motive is driving you today?

10. Write down any other thoughts or feelings that you have today about the question you are discerning.

EXODUS 14:13

Do not be afraid, stand firm, and see the deliverance that the Lord will accomplish for you today.

— Day Ten —

1. Revisit the Question.

2. Begin with a Prayer of Gratitude.

for the times God has guided you in the past.

3. Gut Check.

What are you leaning towards today?   **YES** ☐   **NO** ☐

4. Are you experiencing Consolation or Desolation Today?

Does your soul feel   **LIGHT**   or   **HEAVY**   today?

☐ **CONSOLATION**

☐ **DESOLATION**

5. Feelings.

What is your dominant emotion today?

6. Heart.

What is your heart telling you to do?

7. Mind.

What is your mind telling you to do?

8. Direction.

Do you feel like you are running toward something or away from something?

9. Motive.

What motive is driving you today?

10. Write down any other thoughts or feelings that you have today about the question you are discerning.

Freedom

Are you free? Do you feel free to decide either way?
If not, why not? If you are not free to say no,
you are not free to say yes (and vice versa).

Procrastination

What are you pretending not to know?
Are you procrastinating? Do you already know
what you are called to do in this situation?
Are you pretending not to know?

— Day Eleven —

1. Revisit the Question.

2. Begin with a Prayer of Gratitude.

for the times God has guided you in the past.

3. Gut Check.

What are you leaning towards today?   YES ☐   NO ☐

4. Are you experiencing Consolation or Desolation Today?

Does your soul feel **LIGHT** *or* **HEAVY**   today?

☐ **CONSOLATION**

☐ **DESOLATION**

5. Feelings.

What is your dominant emotion today?

6. Heart.

What is your heart telling you to do?

7. Mind

What is your mind telling you to do?

8. Direction.

Do you feel like you are running toward something or away from something?

9. Motive.

What motive is driving you today?

10. Write down any other thoughts or feelings that you have today about the question you are discerning.

— Day Twelve —

1. Revisit the Question.

2. Begin with a Prayer of Gratitude.

for the times God has guided you in the past.

3. Gut Check.

What are you leaning towards today?   **YES** ☐   **NO** ☐

4. Are you experiencing Consolation or Desolation Today?

Does your soul feel   **LIGHT**   *or*   **HEAVY**   today?

☐ **CONSOLATION**

☐ **DESOLATION**

5. Feelings.

What is your dominant emotion today?

6. Heart.

What is your heart telling you to do?

7. Mind.

What is your mind telling you to do?

8. Direction.

Do you feel like you are running toward something or away from something?

9. Motive.

What motive is driving you today?

10. Write down any other thoughts or feelings that you have today about the question you are discerning.

God is love, and those who abide in love abide in God, and God abides in them.

— Day Thirteen —

1. Revisit the Question.

2. Begin with a Prayer of Gratitude.

for the times God has guided you in the past.

3. Gut Check.

What are you leaning towards today?   YES ☐   NO ☐

4. Are you experiencing Consolation or Desolation Today?

Does your soul feel   **LIGHT**   or   **HEAVY**   today?

☐ **CONSOLATION**

☐ **DESOLATION**

5. Feelings.

What is your dominant emotion today?

6. Heart.

What is your heart telling you to do?

7. Mind

What is your mind telling you to do?

8. Direction.

Do you feel like you are running toward something or away from something?

9. Motive.

What motive is driving you today?

10. Write down any other thoughts or feelings that you have today about the question you are discerning.

— Day Fourteen —

1. Revisit the Question.

2. Begin with a Prayer of Gratitude.

for the times God has guided you in the past.

3. Gut Check.

What are you leaning towards today?   YES ☐   NO ☐

4. Are you experiencing Consolation or Desolation Today?

Does your soul feel   **LIGHT**   *or*   **HEAVY**   today?

☐ **CONSOLATION**

☐ **DESOLATION**

5. Feelings.

What is your dominant emotion today?

6. Heart.

What is your heart telling you to do?

7. Mind.

What is your mind telling you to do?

_____

_____

_____

8. Direction.

Do you feel like you are running toward something or away from something?

_____

_____

_____

9. Motive.

What motive is driving you today?

_____

_____

_____

10. Write down any other thoughts or feelings that you have today about the question you are discerning.

_____

_____

_____

— Day Fifteen —

1. Revisit the Question.

2. Begin with a Prayer of Gratitude.

for the times God has guided you in the past.

3. Gut Check.

What are you leaning towards today?   YES ☐   NO ☐

4. Are you experiencing Consolation or Desolation Today?

Does your soul feel   **LIGHT**   or   **HEAVY**   today?

☐ **CONSOLATION**

☐ **DESOLATION**

5. Feelings.

What is your dominant emotion today? ....

....

....

....

6. Heart.

What is your heart telling you to do? ....

....

....

....

7. Mind.

What is your mind telling you to do?

8. Direction.

Do you feel like you are running toward something or away from something?

9. Motive.

What motive is driving you today?

10. Write down any other thoughts or feelings that you have today about the question you are discerning.

DEUTERONOMY 30:20

Loving the Lord your God, obeying him, and holding fast to him; for that means life to you and length of days.

— Day Sixteen —

1 SAMUEL 12:24

Only fear the Lord, and serve him faithfully with all your heart; for consider what great things he has done for you.

1. Revisit the Question.

2. Begin with a Prayer of Gratitude.

for the times God has guided you in the past.

3. Gut Check.

What are you leaning towards today?   YES ☐   NO ☐

4. Are you experiencing Consolation or Desolation Today?

Does your soul feel   **LIGHT**   *or*   **HEAVY**   today?

☐ **CONSOLATION**

☐ **DESOLATION**

5. Feelings.

What is your dominant emotion today?

6. Heart.

What is your heart telling you to do?

7. Mind.

What is your mind telling you to do?

8. Direction.

Do you feel like you are running toward something or away from something?

9. Motive.

What motive is driving you today?

10. Write down any other thoughts or feelings that you have today about the question you are discerning.

— Day Seventeen —

1. Revisit the Question.

2. Begin with a Prayer of Gratitude.

for the times God has guided you in the past.

3. Gut Check.

What are you leaning towards today?   YES ☐   NO ☐

4. Are you experiencing Consolation or Desolation Today?

Does your soul feel   **LIGHT**   or   **HEAVY**   today?

☐ **CONSOLATION**

☐ **DESOLATION**

5. Feelings.

What is your dominant emotion today?

6. Heart.

What is your heart telling you to do?

7. Mind.

What is your mind telling you to do?

8. Direction.

Do you feel like you are running toward something or away from something?

9. Motive.

What motive is driving you today?

10. Write down any other thoughts or feelings that you have today about the question you are discerning.

1 PETER 3:5

Always be ready to make your defense to anyone who demands from you an accounting for the hope that is in you.

Humble yourselves therefore under the mighty hand of God, so that he may exalt you in due time.

— Day Eighteen —

1. Revisit the Question.

2. Begin with a Prayer of Gratitude.

for the times God has guided you in the past.

3. Gut Check.

What are you leaning towards today?   YES ☐   NO ☐

4. Are you experiencing Consolation or Desolation Today?

Does your soul feel   **LIGHT**   *or*   **HEAVY**   today?

☐ **CONSOLATION**

☐ **DESOLATION**

5. Feelings.

What is your dominant emotion today?

6. Heart.

What is your heart telling you to do?

7. Mind.

What is your mind telling you to do?

8. Direction.

Do you feel like you are running toward something or away from something?

9. Motive.

What motive is driving you today?

10. Write down any other thoughts or feelings that you have today about the question you are discerning.

— Day Nineteen —

1. Revisit the Question.

2. Begin with a Prayer of Gratitude.

for the times God has guided you in the past.

3. Gut Check.

What are you leaning towards today?   YES ☐   NO ☐

4. Are you experiencing Consolation or Desolation today?

Does your soul feel   **LIGHT**   *or*   **HEAVY**   today?

☐ **CONSOLATION**

☐ **DESOLATION**

5. Feelings.

What is your dominant emotion today?

6. Heart.

What is your heart telling you to do?

7. Mind.

What is your mind telling you to do?

8. Direction.

Do you feel like you are running toward something or away from something?

9. Motive.

What motive is driving you today?

10. Write down any other thoughts or feelings that you have today about the question you are discerning.

1 PETER
1:15-15

Instead, as he who called you is holy, be holy yourselves in all your conduct; for it is written, "You shall be holy, for I am holy."

His divine power has given us everything needed for life and godliness, through the knowledge of him who called us by his own glory and goodness.

— Day Twenty —

1. Revisit the Question.

2. Begin with a Prayer of Gratitude.

for the times God has guided you in the past.

3. Gut Check.

What are you leaning towards today?   YES ☐   NO ☐

4. Are you experiencing Consolation or Desolation Today?

Does your soul feel **LIGHT** *or* **HEAVY** today?

☐ **CONSOLATION**

☐ **DESOLATION**

5. Feelings.

What is your dominant emotion today?

6. Heart.

What is your heart telling you to do?

7. Mind.

What is your mind telling you to do?

8. Direction.

Do you feel like you are running toward something or away from something?

9. Motive.

What motive is driving you today?

10. Write down any other thoughts or feelings that you have today about the question you are discerning:

2 PETER
1:2

May grace and peace be yours in abundance in the knowledge of God and of Jesus our Lord.

— Day Twenty-One —

1. Revisit the Question.

2. Begin with a Prayer of Gratitude.

for the times God has guided you in the past.

3. Gut Check.

What are you leaning towards today?   YES ☐   NO ☐

4. Are you experiencing Consolation or Desolation Today?

Does your soul feel **LIGHT** or **HEAVY** today?

☐ **CONSOLATION**

☐ **DESOLATION**

5. Feelings.

What is your dominant emotion today? ....

....

....

....

6. Heart.

What is your heart telling you to do? ....

....

....

....

7. Mind.

What is your mind telling you to do?

8. Direction.

Do you feel like you are running toward something or away from something?

9. Motive.

What motive is driving you today?

10. Write down any other thoughts or feelings that you have today about the question you are discerning.

2 PETER
3:9

The Lord is not slow about his promise, as some think of slowness, but is patient with you, not wanting any to perish, but all to come to repentance.

— Day Twenty-Two —

1. Revisit the Question.

2. Begin with a Prayer of Gratitude.

for the times God has guided you in the past.

3. Gut Check.

What are you leaning towards today?   YES ☐   NO ☐

4. Are you experiencing Consolation or Desolation Today?

Does your soul feel **LIGHT** _or_ **HEAVY** today?

☐ **CONSOLATION**

☐ **DESOLATION**

5. Feelings.

What is your dominant emotion today?

6. Heart.

What is your heart telling you to do?

7. Mind.

What is your mind telling you to do?

8. Direction.

Do you feel like you are running toward something or away from something?

9. Motive.

What motive is driving you today?

10. Write down any other thoughts or feelings that you have today about the question you are discerning.

NAHUM 1:7

The Lord is good, a stronghold in a day of trouble; he protects those who take refuge in him.

— Day Twenty-Three —

1. Revisit the Question.

2. Begin with a Prayer of Gratitude.

for the times God has guided you in the past.

3. Gut Check.

What are you leaning towards today?　　　YES ☐　　　NO ☐

4. Are you experiencing Consolation or Desolation today?

Does your soul feel **LIGHT** or **HEAVY** today?

☐ **CONSOLATION**

☐ **DESOLATION**

5. Feelings.

What is your dominant emotion today?

6. Heart.

What is your heart telling you to do?

7. Mind.

What is your mind telling you to do?

8. Direction.

Do you feel like you are running toward something or away from something?

9. Motive.

What motive is driving you today?

10. Write down any other thoughts or feelings that you have today about the question you are discerning.

The Lord, your God, is in your midst, a warrior who gives victory; he will rejoice over you with gladness, he will renew you in his love; he will exult over you with loud singing.

— Day Twenty-Four —

ZECHARIAH 8:16

These are the things that you shall do: Speak the truth to one another, render in your gates judgments that are true and make for peace.

1. Revisit the Question.

2. Begin with a Prayer of Gratitude.

for the times God has guided you in the past.

3. Gut Check.

What are you leaning towards today?   YES ☐   NO ☐

4. Are you experiencing Consolation or Desolation today?

Does your soul feel   **LIGHT**   or   **HEAVY**   today?

☐ **CONSOLATION**

☐ **DESOLATION**

5. Feelings.

What is your dominant emotion today?

6. Heart.

What is your heart telling you to do?

7. Mind.

What is your mind telling you to do?

8. Direction.

Do you feel like you are running toward something or away from something?

9. Motive.

What motive is driving you today?

10. Write down any other thoughts or feelings that you have today about the question you are discerning.

MATTHEW
5:14

You are the light of the world. A city built on a hill cannot be hid.

— Day Twenty-Five —

1. Revisit the Question.

2. Begin with a Prayer of Gratitude.

for the times God has guided you in the past.

3. Gut Check.

What are you leaning towards today?   YES ☐   NO ☐

4. Are you experiencing Consolation or Desolation Today?

Does your soul feel   **LIGHT**   *or*   **HEAVY**   today?

☐ **CONSOLATION**

☐ **DESOLATION**

5. Feelings.

What is your dominant emotion today?

6. Heart.

What is your heart telling you to do?

7. Mind.

What is your mind telling you to do?

8. Direction.

Do you feel like you are running toward something or away from something?

9. Motive.

What motive is driving you today?

10. Write down any other thoughts or feelings that you have today about the question you are discerning.

MATTHEW 6:33

But strive first for the kingdom of God and his righteousness, and all these things will be given to you as well.

Evil Spirits

Evil is real. Evil spirits are real.
A quick glance through the history books
makes that abundantly clear. The line that
separates good from evil is cast down the center
of each person's heart. It's a mistake to think too
much about evil spirits, but it is also a mistake to
ignore them altogether. How do you feel evil forces
are affecting you in this process of discernment?

Fear

What are you afraid of in the situation you are discerning?
Are these fears new or recurring fears in your life?
What is driving these fears? What are you really afraid of?
Go deep into your fears, don't pretend they don't exist.
The more you ignore them the more powerful they become.
Face yours fears with God and see them for what they are.

MATTHEW
5:3

Blessed are the poor in spirit, for theirs is the kingdom of heaven.

— Day Twenty-Six —

1. Revisit the Question.

2. Begin with a Prayer of Gratitude.

for the times God has guided you in the past.

3. Gut Check.

What are you leaning towards today?　　**YES** ☐　　　**NO** ☐

4. Are you experiencing Consolation or Desolation today?

Does your soul feel　**LIGHT**　or　**HEAVY**　today?

☐　**CONSOLATION**

☐　**DESOLATION**

5. Feelings.

What is your dominant emotion today?

6. Heart.

What is your heart telling you to do?

7. Mind.

What is your mind telling you to do?

_____

_____

_____

8. Direction.

Do you feel like you are running toward something or away from something?

_____

_____

_____

9. Motive.

What motive is driving you today?

_____

_____

_____

10. Write down any other thoughts or feelings that you have today about the question you are discerning.

_____

_____

_____

— Day Twenty-Seven —

1. Revisit the Question.

2. Begin with a Prayer of Gratitude.

for the times God has guided you in the past.

3. Gut Check.

What are you leaning towards today?   **YES** ☐   **NO** ☐

4. Are you experiencing Consolation or Desolation Today?

Does your soul feel   **LIGHT**   *or*   **HEAVY**   today?

☐ **CONSOLATION**

☐ **DESOLATION**

5. Feelings.

What is your dominant emotion today?

6. Heart.

What is your heart telling you to do?

7. Mind.

What is your mind telling you to do?

8. Direction.

Do you feel like you are running toward something or away from something?

9. Motive.

What motive is driving you today?

10. Write down any other thoughts or feelings that you have today about the question you are discerning.

MATTHEW 5:6

Blessed are those who hunger and thirst for righteousness, for they will be filled.

— Day Twenty-Eight —

1. Revisit the Question.

2. Begin with a Prayer of Gratitude.

for the times God has guided you in the past.

3. Gut Check.

What are you leaning towards today?   YES ☐   NO ☐

4. Are you experiencing Consolation or Desolation Today?

Does your soul feel **LIGHT** or **HEAVY** today?

☐ **CONSOLATION**

☐ **DESOLATION**

5. Feelings.

What is your dominant emotion today? ....

....

....

....

6. Heart.

What is your heart telling you to do? ....

....

....

....

7. Mind.

What is your mind telling you to do?

8. Direction.

Do you feel like you are running toward something or away from something?

9. Motive.

What motive is driving you today?

10. Write down any other thoughts or feelings that you have today about the question you are discerning.

MATTHEW
5:9

Blessed are the peacemakers, for they will be called children of God.

— Day Twenty-Nine —

1. Revisit the Question.

2. Begin with a Prayer of Gratitude.

for the times God has guided you in the past.

3. Gut Check.

What are you leaning towards today?   YES ☐   NO ☐

4. Are you experiencing Consolation or Desolation Today?

Does your soul feel **LIGHT** *or* **HEAVY** today?

☐ **CONSOLATION**

☐ **DESOLATION**

5. Feelings.

What is your dominant emotion today?

6. Heart.

What is your heart telling you to do?

7. Mind.

What is your mind telling you to do?

8. Direction.

Do you feel like you are running toward something or away from something?

9. Motive.

What motive is driving you today?

10. Write down any other thoughts or feelings that you have today about the question you are discerning.

MATTHEW
5:10

Blessed are those who are persecuted for righteousness' sake, for theirs is the kingdom of heaven.

— Day Thirty —

1. Revisit the Question.

2. Begin with a Prayer of Gratitude.

for the times God has guided you in the past.

3. Gut Check.

What are you leaning towards today?   YES ☐   NO ☐

4. Are you experiencing Consolation or Desolation Today?

Does your soul feel   **LIGHT**   *or*   **HEAVY**   today?

☐ **CONSOLATION**

☐ **DESOLATION**

5. Feelings.

What is your dominant emotion today? ....

....

....

....

6. Heart.

What is your heart telling you to do? ....

....

....

....

7. Mind.

What is your mind telling you to do?

8. Direction.

Do you feel like you are running toward something or away from something?

9. Motive.

What motive is driving you today?

10. Write down any other thoughts or feelings that you have today about the question you are discerning.

— Day Thirty-One —

1. Revisit the Question.

2. Begin with a Prayer of Gratitude.

for the times God has guided you in the past.

3. Gut Check.

What are you leaning towards today?   YES ☐   NO ☐

4. Are you experiencing Consolation or Desolation Today?

Does your soul feel   **LIGHT**   *or*   **HEAVY**   today?

☐ **CONSOLATION**

☐ **DESOLATION**

5. Feelings.

What is your dominant emotion today?

6. Heart.

What is your heart telling you to do?

7. Mind.

What is your mind telling you to do?

8. Direction.

Do you feel like you are running toward something or away from something?

9. Motive.

What motive is driving you today?

10. Write down any other thoughts or feelings that you have today about the question you are discerning.

MATTHEW
6:24

No one can serve two masters; for a slave will either hate the one and love the other, or be devoted to the one and despise the other. You cannot serve God and wealth.

MATTHEW 5:16

In the same way, let your light shine before others, so that they may see your good works and give glory to your Father in heaven.

— Day Thirty-Two —

1. Revisit the Question.

2. Begin with a Prayer of Gratitude.
for the times God has guided you in the past.

3. Gut Check.
What are you leaning towards today?   YES ☐   NO ☐

4. Are you experiencing Consolation or Desolation Today?
Does your soul feel **LIGHT** *or* **HEAVY** today?

☐ **CONSOLATION**

☐ **DESOLATION**

5. Feelings.
What is your dominant emotion today?

6. Heart.
What is your heart telling you to do?

7. Mind.

What is your mind telling you to do?

8. Direction.

Do you feel like you are running toward something or away from something?

9. Motive.

What motive is driving you today?

10. Write down any other thoughts or feelings that you have today about the question you are discerning.

"You have heard that it was said, 'You shall love your neighbor and hate your enemy.'
But I say to you, Love your enemies and pray for those who persecute you."

— Day Thirty-Three —

1. Revisit the Question.

2. Begin with a Prayer of Gratitude.

for the times God has guided you in the past.

3. Gut Check.

What are you leaning towards today?　　　YES ☐　　　　NO ☐

4. Are you experiencing Consolation or Desolation Today?

Does your soul feel　**LIGHT**　*or*　**HEAVY**　today?

☐　**CONSOLATION**

☐　**DESOLATION**

5. Feelings.

What is your dominant emotion today?

6. Heart.

What is your heart telling you to do?

7. Mind.

What is your mind telling you to do?

8. Direction.

Do you feel like you are running toward something or away from something?

9. Motive.

What motive is driving you today?

10. Write down any other thoughts or feelings that you have today about the question you are discerning.

MATTHEW 18:20

For where two or three are gathered in my name, I am there among them.

— Day Thirty-Four —

MARK
9:23

Jesus said to him, "If you are able!–All things can be done for the one who believes."

1. Revisit the Question.

2. Begin with a Prayer of Gratitude.

for the times God has guided you in the past.

3. Gut Check.

What are you leaning towards today?   YES ☐   NO ☐

4. Are you experiencing Consolation or Desolation today?

Does your soul feel   **LIGHT**   *or*   **HEAVY**   today?

☐ **CONSOLATION**

☐ **DESOLATION**

5. Feelings.

What is your dominant emotion today?

6. Heart.

What is your heart telling you to do?

7. Mind.

What is your mind telling you to do?

8. Direction.

Do you feel like you are running toward something or away from something?

9. Motive.

What motive is driving you today?

10. Write down any other thoughts or feelings that you have today about the question you are discerning.

MARK
12:30

You shall love the Lord your God with all your heart, and with all your soul, and with all your mind, and with all your strength.

And Jesus said to them, "Follow me and I will make you fish for people."

— Day Thirty-Five —

1. Revisit the Question.

2. Begin with a Prayer of Gratitude.

for the times God has guided you in the past.

3. Gut Check.

What are you leaning towards today?   **YES** ☐   **NO** ☐

4. Are you experiencing Consolation or Desolation Today?

Does your soul feel **LIGHT** *or* **HEAVY** today?

☐ **CONSOLATION**

☐ **DESOLATION**

5. Feelings.

What is your dominant emotion today?

6. Heart.

What is your heart telling you to do?

7. Mind

What is your mind telling you to do?

8. Direction.

Do you feel like you are running toward something or away from something?

9. Motive.

What motive is driving you today?

10. Write down any other thoughts or feelings that you have today about the question you are discerning.

MARK
11:24

Listen! I am standing at the door, knocking; if you hear my voice and open the door, I will come in to you and eat with you, and you with me.

— Day Thirty-Six —

REVELATION
3:20

Listen! I am standing at the door, knocking; if you hear my voice and open the door, I will come in to you and eat with you, and you with me.

1. Revisit the Question.

2. Begin with a Prayer of Gratitude.

for the times God has guided you in the past.

3. Gut Check.

What are you leaning towards today?   YES ☐   NO ☐

4. Are you experiencing Consolation or Desolation Today?

Does your soul feel   **LIGHT**   or   **HEAVY**   today?

☐ **CONSOLATION**

☐ **DESOLATION**

5. Feelings.

What is your dominant emotion today?

6. Heart.

What is your heart telling you to do?

7. Mind

What is your mind telling you to do?

8. Direction.

Do you feel like you are running toward something or away from something?

9. Motive.

What motive is driving you today?

10. Write down any other thoughts or feelings that you have today about the question you are discerning.

— Day Thirty-Seven —

MARK
11:25

Whenever you stand praying, forgive, if you have anything against anyone;
so that your Father in heaven may also forgive you your trespasses.

1. Revisit the Question.

2. Begin with a Prayer of Gratitude.

for the times God has guided you in the past.

3. Gut Check.

What are you leaning towards today?   YES ☐   NO ☐

4. Are you experiencing Consolation or Desolation Today?

Does your soul feel   **LIGHT**   or   **HEAVY**   today?

☐ **CONSOLATION**

☐ **DESOLATION**

5. Feelings.

What is your dominant emotion today?

6. Heart.

What is your heart telling you to do?

7. Mind.

What is your mind telling you to do?

8. Direction.

Do you feel like you are running toward something or away from something?

9. Motive.

What motive is driving you today?

10. Write down any other thoughts or feelings that you have today about the question you are discerning.

REVELATION 3:8

Look, I have set before you an open door, which no one is able to shut.

— Day Thirty-Eight —

1. Revisit the Question.

2. Begin with a Prayer of Gratitude.

for the times God has guided you in the past.

3. Gut Check.

What are you leaning towards today?   YES ☐   NO ☐

4. Are you experiencing Consolation or Desolation Today?

Does your soul feel **LIGHT** *or* **HEAVY** today?

☐ **CONSOLATION**

☐ **DESOLATION**

5. Feelings.

What is your dominant emotion today?

6. Heart.

What is your heart telling you to do?

7. Mind.

What is your mind telling you to do?

8. Direction.

Do you feel like you are running toward something or away from something?

9. Motive.

What motive is driving you today?

10. Write down any other thoughts or feelings that you have today about the question you are discerning.

HEBREWS
11:1

Now faith is the assurance of things hoped for, the conviction of things not seen.

— Day Thirty-Nine —

1. Revisit the Question.

2. Begin with a Prayer of Gratitude.

for the times God has guided you in the past.

3. Gut Check.

What are you leaning towards today?   **YES** ☐   **NO** ☐

4. Are you experiencing Consolation or Desolation Today?

Does your soul feel **LIGHT** *or* **HEAVY** today?

☐ **CONSOLATION**

☐ **DESOLATION**

5. Feelings.

What is your dominant emotion today? ....

....

....

....

6. Heart.

What is your heart telling you to do? ....

....

....

....

7. Mind.

What is your mind telling you to do?

8. Direction.

Do you feel like you are running toward something or away from something?

9. Motive.

What motive is driving you today?

10. Write down any other thoughts or feelings that you have today about the question you are discerning.

— Day Forty —

1. Revisit the Question.

2. Begin with a Prayer of Gratitude.

for the times God has guided you in the past.

3. Gut Check.

What are you leaning towards today?   **YES** ☐   **NO** ☐

4. Are you experiencing Consolation or Desolation Today?

Does your soul feel   **LIGHT**   *or*   **HEAVY**   today?

☐ **CONSOLATION**

☐ **DESOLATION**

5. Feelings.

What is your dominant emotion today?

6. Heart.

What is your heart telling you to do?

7. Mind.

What is your mind telling you to do?

8. Direction.

Do you feel like you are running toward something or away from something?

9. Motive.

What motive is driving you today?

10. Write down any other thoughts or feelings that you have today about the question you are discerning.

JAMES
1:22

But be doers of the word, and not merely hearers who deceive themselves.

Enthusiasm

The Spirit of God often fills us with enthusiasm.
What excites you about deciding in one way
or another the question you are discerning?
What excites you about the other direction?

Part Five:

Dreaming With God

SOMETHING WONDERFUL IS ABOUT TO HAPPEN!

Dreams play a fabulous role in our lives. Dreaming is one of the few things we do while we are both asleep and awake. Our sleeping dreams and our waking dreams may be very different, but both play powerful roles in our lives. Our sleeping dreams very often reveal our deepest unconscious, while few things are more conscious and intentional than our waking dreams.

Throughout the Scriptures we read about God and his angels speaking to people in their sleeping dreams, and yet we often doubt God's role and presence in our waking dreams.

As human beings we have been endowed with many awe-inspiring gifts. First among them is life itself. It is a miracle and wonder in all its forms, but life is uniquely miraculous in its human expression. Next and second among the astounding gifts God has given human beings is the gift of free will—the ability to say " I will do this" and "I will not do that."

We speak often about life and free will, but the third gift is often neglected. It is the ability to dream. We have been given the ability to look into the future, imagine something bigger and better, and then return to the present and work to bring about that richly imagined future. Few human abilities are more extraordinary.

To dream is a God-given ability, and yet, too often, we let it languish unemployed in the corner of our lives.

God speaks to us in the Scriptures, he speaks to us through other people, he speaks to us through nature, and he speaks to us through the circumstances of our lives. And he speaks to us through our deepest desires.

God has placed good desires deep in your heart. Through prayer and reflection we dig them up, dust them off, and learn to cherish them. One of the reasons we struggle to chase the dreams God has placed deep in our hearts is because the world fills our hearts with so many shallow and superficial desires. This is often why we are unable to answer the simple question: What do you want?

Prayer and reflection empower us to dig through these shallow, superficial desires and get to our deepest desires. It is only then that we discover that all along, though we were perhaps unaware of it, we have wanted what God wants. When our desires align with God's desires it is then that we experience a spiritual ecstasy beyond compare.

In the following pages you will find a series of questions designed to help you reconnect with your God-given ability to dream. Write down your answers. Don't edit yourself. Don't judge your dreams. Your dreams are your dreams for a reason. Write them down and date them.

Perhaps you have stopped dreaming. That's okay. There is no time better than right now to realize that. Maybe you stopped dreaming because you had a dream that was crushed or lost. Or maybe you obsessed about one dream for so long and by the time you accomplished that dream, you had forgotten how to dream.

Whatever may be the case, begin dreaming again today. God has given you this powerful gift for a reason.

Once you are finished dreaming your dreams and answering your questions, I would like you to look back over the dreams you have written on these pages and reflect on two questions: How much money would I need to pay you to give up on your dreams? What sacrifices are you willing to make to achieve them?

Dream. Dream. This is a time to dream. For when we dream, we are reminded that better days are yet to come. It is when we pray and dream that we see all the beauty that is within us and around us. Praying and dreaming allows God to remind us of all that is possible.

Blessed is anyone who endures temptation. Such a one has stood the test and will receive the crown of life that the Lord has promised to those who love him.

1.

What is something you did as a child that you would like to do again?

2.

If you could have lunch with any living person, who would you want to have lunch with?

3.

What language would you like to learn?

4.

What fear do you dream of overcoming?

5.

If you could improve any one aspect of your home,
what would you choose?

6.

If you could have front row tickets to any show,
which would you choose?

JAMES 1:17   Every generous act of giving, with every perfect gift, is from above, coming down from the Father of lights, with whom there is no variation or shadow due to change.

7.

What spiritual habit would you like to develop?

8.

If you could learn to play any musical instrument, which would you choose?

9.

What hobby have you always wanted to explore?

10.

Which of your talents would you like to develop more?

11.

If you were at optimum health,
how would you look and feel differently?

12.

What virtue do you want to exemplify in your life?

JUDE
1:21

Keep yourselves in the love of God; look forward to the mercy of our Lord Jesus Christ that leads to eternal life.

13.

Which person from your childhood would you most like to reconnect with?

14.

Which relationship would you most like to improve?

15.

What city would you like to live in for six months?

16.

If you could own any car, what would you choose?

17.

What physical activity would you like to do more often?

18.

If you could meet any five people from any time in history,
whom would you want to meet?

And this is love, that we walk according to his commandments; this is the commandment just as you have heard it from the beginning—you must walk in it.

19.

What addiction would you like to be free from, and how would that change your life?

20.

What is your dream job?

21.

If you could vacation any five places in the world,
where would you go?

_____

_____

_____

_____

22.

How many hours of sleep do you need to be at your best?

_____

_____

23.

Which broken relationship would you like to repair or improve?

_____

_____

_____

_____

24.

If you were going to write a book, what would you write about?

25.

What one quality would you like your team at work to work on?

26.

In what one way would you like your
primary relationship to change?

....

....

....

27.

Which coach, teacher, or mentor, do you want to emulate?

....

....

28.

What do you want to learn about yourself?

....

....

....

EPHESIANS
2:8

For by grace you have been saved through faith, and this is not your own doing; it is the gift of God.

As God's chosen ones, holy and beloved, clothe yourselves with compassion, kindness, humility, meekness, and patience.

29.

How much money do you want to save next year?

30.

What do you want your children to say about you?

31.

What would a perfect day be for you?

32.

If you could change one thing about your workspace, what would you change?

_____

_____

_____

_____

33.

If you could take a road trip with anyone and go anywhere, where would you go and who would you go with?

_____

_____

_____

_____

34.

What skill, talent, or ability would you like to possess?

_____

_____

_____

_____

COLOSSIANS
3:2

Set your minds on things that are above, not on things that are on earth.

#35.

In what ways do you dream of simplifying your life?

#36.

If someone gave you $1,000 and you had to spend it today, what would buy?

#37.

What one virtue would you like to be known and respected for?

#38.

What hobby do you dream of spending more time enjoying?

#39.

What would your perfect weekend look like . . . where would you go? What would you do? Who would you be with?

#40.

In what way do you dream of being more comfortable with yourself?

41.

If you could be an expert in anything, what would it be?

42.

What do you want the last words you speak to be?

43.

If you could hang any artwork in your home by any artist, who would you choose?

44.

If you could go back to school to study anything, what would you choose?

45.

What would you do if you had unlimited resources?

LUKE
9:62

Jesus said to him, "No one who puts a hand to the plow and looks back is fit for the kingdom of God."

46.

*If there were a movie about your life,
what would be the most interesting parts?*

In reply he said to them, "Whoever has two coats must share with anyone who has none; and whoever has food must do likewise."

47.

Who do you most want to express your gratitude to?

48.

What organization, cause, or charity do you dream of supporting more?

49.

If you were full of courage, what would you do?

50.

What qualities do you want others to remember you for?

51.

What do you want your legacy to be?

LUKE 1:9

So I say to you, ask, and it will be given you; search, and you will find; knock, and the door will be opened for you.

Who you become
is infinitely more
important than
what you do,
or what you have.

From *The Rhythm of Life*

"The people we surround ourselves with either raise
or lower our standards.
They either help us to become
the-best-version-of-ourselves
or encourage us to become
lesser versions of ourselves.
We become like our friends.
No man becomes great on his
own. No woman becomes great on
her own. The people around them
help to make them great. We all
need people in our lives who raise
our standards, remind us of our
essential purpose,
and challenge us to become
the-best-version-of-ourselves."

From *The Rhythm of Life*

"

There are many
paths you can
choose to follow
both personally
and professionally.
You don't have to
settle for the life you
stumbled into.

From *Off Balance*

"

Freedom is not
the ability to do
whatever you
want. Freedom
is the strength of
character to do
what is good, true,
noble, and right.

From *The Seven Levels of Intimacy*